A Little Book of

A Little Book of

Courage

Ruskin Bond

SPEAKING
TIGER

SPEAKING TIGER PUBLISHING PVT. LTD
4381/4 Ansari Road, Daryaganj,
New Delhi–110002, India

ISBN: 978-93-88070-08-9
eISBN: 978-93-88070-07-2

10 9 8 7 6 5 4 3 2 1

Typeset in Garamond Pro by SÜRYA, New Delhi
Printed at Thomson Press, Delhi

SPEAKING TIGER PUBLISHING PVT. LTD
4381/4 Ansari Road, Daryaganj,
New Delhi–110002, India

Anthology copyright © Speaking Tiger 2018
Introduction copyright © Ruskin Bond 2018

ISBN: 978-93-88070-06-5
eISBN: 978-93-88070-07-2

10 9 8 7 6 5 4 3 2 1

Typeset in Garamond Pro by SŪRYA, New Delhi
Printed at Thomson Press, Delhi

Introduction

''Tisn't life that matters, but the courage you bring to it.'

This is the opening line of Hugh Walpole's novel *Fortitude*, which no one reads today, but which made a great impression on me when I was twelve. Its young hero grows up to become a successful writer, and I intended to do the same. You need courage to do the things you have set your heart upon, and you need courage to overcome the failures and disappointments that are bound to come your way, to put them behind you, and to carry on till you have reached the end of the road you have chosen. And 'the road less chosen' is probably the most difficult, because it is a lonely road.

'Never despair. But if you do, then work on in despair.'

This is another line that I have carried about in my head since my schooldays. I don't remember who said it, but I have often repeated it to young writers (and others) who have done their best, and failed, and are about to give up in their quest for glory or whatever it is that they want to achieve. You don't give up. You try again. Fail again. Keep failing. Keep trying. Something will come out of it.

Courage, my friend. Courage to the end.

Because it *is* life that matters. Most of us want to live, even if we come into this world in the most dreadful of circumstances—born in a slum, or in a war zone, or born unwanted...But like birds, we desire to fly. Like ants, we build our anthills. Like moles, we protect our burrows. Like owls, we learn to live in the dark. Like minnows, we seek calm waters.

We defend our own peculiar way of life, and when it is threatened, we resist. When someone wishes to impose his will, his way of life on us, we may take a long time to stand up to him, but we finally do. The conquerors are defeated. Alexander succumbs. Ceasar is undone. Napoleon is exiled. Hitler melts into madness. Mankind is the victor!

Courage, my friend. May it last you to the end. And may this little book be your companion on the journey.

Ruskin Bond

Landour, July 2018

(Publisher's note: All quotes in the book that are not attributed to anyone are by Ruskin Bond.)

There is no dream which may
not come true
if we have the energy which
determines our own fate.

Life is mostly froth and bubble,
Two things stand like stone.
Kindness in another's trouble,
Courage in your own.
—*Adam Lindsay Gordon*

Be like water, taught Lao-tzu. Soft and limpid, it finds its way through, over or under any obstacle. It does not quarrel; it simply moves on.

To persevere takes the greatest courage.

❧

The most fundamental
aggression to ourselves, the most
fundamental harm we can do to
ourselves, is to remain ignorant
by not having the courage and
the respect to look at ourselves
honestly and gently.

—Pema Chödrön

My window-sill allows me just enough space to grow a few flowering plants: Geraniums, bright red or salmon-pink; nasturtiums; and, in winter, chrysanthemums. They keep my spirits from faltering. Every writer needs a few flowers to keep him going.

❧

Keep right on to the end of the road,
Keep right on to the end.
If your way be long,
Let your heart be strong,
So keep right on to the end.

—*Harry Lauder*

When things go wrong, as they
sometimes will,
When the road you're trudging
seems all uphill,
When the funds are low but the
debts are high,
And you want to smile but you
have to sigh,
When care is pressing you down
a bit,
Rest if you must, but don't you
quit!

   —Edgar A. Guest

May your trails be crooked, winding, lonesome, dangerous, leading to the most amazing view. May your mountains rise into and above the clouds.

—*Edward Abbey*

Notes

_____

_____

_____

_____

_____

_____

_____

_____

_____

_____

_____

_____

.18.

_____

_____

_____

_____

_____

_____

_____

_____

_____

_____

_____

_____

_____

_____

_____

_____

_____

.Ruskin Bond.

_.19._

❧

.Ruskin Bond.

Leap, and the net will appear.

—John Burroughs

That small red ant striding
along may mean nothing to an
indifferent world, but to me
it represents industry, single-
mindedness—a dogged bravery.

.Ruskin Bond.

You stride through the long grass,
Pressing on over fallen pine
needles,
Up the winding road to the
mountain pass:
Small red ant, now crossing a sea
Of raindrops; your destiny
To carry home that single, slender
Cosmos seed,

Waving it like a banner in the sun.

❧

Fortitude is the marshal of
thought, the armor of the will,
and the fort of reason.

—*Francis Bacon*

Oh, a trouble's a ton, or a
trouble's an ounce,
Or a trouble is what you make it,
And it isn't the fact that you're
hurt that counts,
But only how did you take it?

—*Ray Kinard*

The slender maidenhair fern
grows firm on a rock,
While all around her the water
swirls and chatters
And then disappears in a rush
Down to the bottom of the hill.
When I'm surrounded by
troubled waters, Lord,
Let me find within a rock to
cling to,
And give me the quiet patience
of the maidenhair
Who has learned to live with the
rock.

❧

If your determination is fixed, I do not counsel you to despair. Few things are impossible to diligence and skill. Great works are performed not by strength, but perseverance.

—*Samuel Johnson*

Faith. You can do very little with it, but you can do nothing without it.

—*Samuel Butler*

Children on their way to school
in Garhwal:

Five more miles to go!
We climb through rain and snow.
A river to cross...
A mountain to pass...
Now we've four more miles to go.

❧

Stand like a beaten anvil, when thy dream
Is laid upon thee, golden from the fire.
Flinch not, though heavily through that furnace-gleam
The black forge-hammers fall on thy desire.

—*Alfred Noyes*

Notes

❧

.30.

.Ruskin Bond.

_____

_____

_____

_____

_____

_____

_____

_____

_____

_____   *.31.*

_____

_____

_____

_____

_____

_____

_____

❧

＊

.Ruskin Bond.

Never bend your head.
Always hold it high.
Look the world straight in the eye.

—Helen Keller

No one can make you feel inferior
without your consent.

—*Eleanor Roosevelt*

❧

The simple step of a courageous
individual is not to take part
in the lie. 'One word of truth
outweighs the world.'

—*Aleksandr Solzhenitsyn*

❧

The only tyrant I accept in this world is the 'still small voice' within me. And even though I have to face the prospect of being a minority of one, I humbly believe I have the courage to be in such a hopeless minority.

—*Mahatma Gandhi*

❧

You will have to make up
for the smallness of your size
by your courage and selfless
devotion to duty, for it is not life
that matters, but the courage,
fortitude and determination you
bring to it.

—*Muhammad Ali Jinnah*

❧

Hold on to your dreams,
      and don't let go!
Follow the rainbow,
The tide in its flow,
Salute the sun
      at the break of day
Find time for the flowers
      along the way
Follow the birds
      as they come and go.
Hold on to your dreams,
      and don't let go!

I am only one,
But still I am one.
I cannot do everything,
But still I can do something;
And because I cannot do
everything,
I will not refuse to do the
something that I can do.

38.
—*Edward Everett Hale*

Impossible is just a word thrown around by small men who find it easier to live in the world they've been given than to explore the power they have to change it. Impossible is not a fact. It's an opinion. Impossible is potential. Impossible is temporary. Impossible is nothing.

—*Muhammad Ali*

Everyday courage has few witnesses. But yours is no less noble because no drum beats for you and no crowds shout your name.

—*Robert Louis Stevenson*

Notes

_____

_____

_____

_____

_____

.41.

_____

_____

_____

_____

_____

_____

_____

🌱

.Ruskin Bond.

_____

_____

_____

_____

_____

_____

_____

_____

_____

_____   .43.

_____

_____

_____

_____

_____

_____

_____

❧

.44.

_____

_____

_____

_____

_____

_____

_____

_____

_____

_____

_____

_____

_____

_____

_____

❧

.Ruskin Bond.

The man who moves a mountain
begins by carrying away small stones.

—Confucius

A great book begins with an idea;
a great life, with a determination.

—*Louis L'Amour*

For all your days prepare,
And meet them ever alike:
When you are the anvil, bear—
When you are the hammer, strike.

—*Edwin Markham*

Risk! Risk anything! Care no
more for the opinions of others,
for those voices. Do the hardest
thing on earth for you. Act for
yourself. Face the truth.

—*Katherine Mansfield*

Luck is a very good word if you put a P before it.

—*Anonymous*

A ship is safe in harbor, but that's not what ships are for.

—*John A. Shedd*

March, the Channel was foggy and the sea choppy. I suddenly realized that for the first time in my life I was really and truly on my own. No parents to back me, no relatives to fall back on. Alone. All by myself in a wilderness of wind and water. The way I wanted it. Eighteen, and in control of my own destiny.

❧

Twenty years from now you will be more disappointed by the things that you didn't do than by the ones you did do. So throw off the bowlines. Sail away from the safe harbor. Catch the trade winds in your sails. Explore. Dream. Discover.

—*H. Jackson Brown Jr.*

.Ruskin Bond.

Only the timid and the weak
leave things to destiny (daivam)
but the strong and the self-
confident never bank on destiny
or luck (bhagya).

—The Bhagavad Gita

Many strokes, though with a
little axe,
Hew down and fell the hardest-
timber'd oak.

—*William Shakespeare*

This hill though high I covent
ascend;
The difficulty will not me offend;
For I perceive the way of life lies
here.
Come, pluck up, heart; let's
neither faint nor fear.

—*John Bunyan*

❧

Notes

_____

_____

_____

_____

_____

_____

_____

_____

_____

_____

_____

❧

_.54._

.Ruskin Bond.

_____

_____

_____

_____

_____

_____

_____

_____

_____

_____   *.55.*

_____

_____

_____

_____

_____

_____

_____

❧

.56.

.Ruskin Bond.

Destiny, really, is merely the strength of one's desires.

I learned that courage was not the absence of fear, but the triumph over it. The brave man is not he who does not feel afraid, but he who conquers that fear.

—*Nelson Mandela*

The ultimate measure of a man is not where he stands in moments of comfort and convenience, but where he stands at times of challenge and controversy. The true neighbor will risk his position, his prestige and even his life for the welfare of others.

—*Martin Luther King Jr.*

❧

One of the duties of fortitude is to keep the weak from receiving injury; another, to check the wrong motions of our own souls; a third, both to disregard humiliations, and to do what is right with an even mind.

—*Saint Ambrose*

Out of the night that covers me,
Black as the Pit from pole to pole,
I thank whatever gods may be
For my unconquerable soul…

It matters not how strait the gate,
How charged with punishments
the scroll,
I am the master of my fate:
I am the captain of my soul.

—*William E. Henley*

🌿

If you can keep your head when
all about you
Are losing theirs and blaming it
on you,
If you can trust yourself when all
men doubt you,
But make allowance for their
doubting too;
If you can wait and not be tired
by waiting,

Or being lied about, don't deal
in lies,
Or being hated, don't give way to
hating,
And yet don't look too good, nor
talk too wise...
Yours is the Earth and everything
that's in it.

                    —*Rudyard Kipling*

If the Sun and Moon
should doubt,
They'd immediately go out.
—*William Blake*

Without courage you can't
practice any other virtue
consistently. You can practice any
virtue erratically, but nothing
consistently without courage.
—*Maya Angelou*

.63.

Happy the man, and happy he alone,
He, who can all today his own;
He who, secure within, can say:
'Tomorrow, do thy worst, for I have liv'd today.'

—*Horace*

Notes

_____

_____

_____

_____

_____

_____

_____

_____

_____

_____

_____

_____

.65.

.66.

_____

_____

_____

_____

_____

_____

_____

_____

_____

_____

_____

_____

_____

_____

_____

_____

.Ruskin Bond.

_____

_____

_____

_____

_____

_____

_____

_____

_____

_____ .67.

_____

_____

_____

_____

_____

_____

_____

❧

.Ruskin Bond.

When you are down and out,
Lift up your head and shout—
It's going to be a great day!

The most courageous act is still
to think for yourself. Aloud.

—*Coco Chanel*

Sometimes all we need is a children's rhyme to teach us when to stay the course, and when not:

'For every ailment under the sun,
There is a remedy, or there is none;
If there be one, try to find it;
If there be none, never mind it.'

.71.

❧

Never underestimate the power of the underdog. Shakespeare, the great bard himself celebrates one with these immortal words:

'That's a valiant flea that dare eat his breakfast on the lip of a lion.'

And at times, discretion is the better part of valour. As the poet Ogden Nash eloquently expresses:

'Should you behold a panther crouch,
Prepare to say Ouch.
Better yet, if called by a panther,
Don't anther.'

❧

Village folk have always advised me to run downhill if chased by a bear. They say bears find it easier to run uphill than down. In all these years, I have yet to be chased by one, and am quite happy. Uphill or downhill, a wild bear is best given a very wide path.

.Ruskin Bond.

Notes

_____

_____

_____

_____

_____

_____

_____

_____

_____

_____

_____

_____

_____

.Ruskin Bond.

✤

.A Little Book of Courage.

❧

.Ruskin Bond.

When one door closes,
another door opens.
Take heart.

Be still, sad heart, and cease
repining,
Behind the clouds the sun is
shining;
Thy fate is the common fate of all;
Into each life some rain must
fall,—
Some days must be dark and
dreary.

     —H.W. Longfellow

    ❧

Letting go takes a lot of courage sometimes. But once you let go, happiness comes very quickly. You won't have to go around to search for it.

—*Thich Nhat Hanh*

Have enough courage to trust love one more time and always one more time.

—*Maya Angelou*

To do the useful thing, to
say the courageous thing, to
contemplate the beautiful thing:
that is enough for one man's life.
—*T.S. Eliot*

For life is the mirror of king and
slave,
'Tis just what we are and do;
Then give to the world the best
you have
And the best will come back to
you.
—*Madeline S. Bridges*

All men have their frailties; and whoever looks for a friend without imperfections will never find what he seeks. We love ourselves notwithstanding our faults, and we ought to love our friends in like manner.

—*Cyrus*

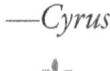

Being deeply loved by someone gives you strength; loving someone deeply gives you courage.

—*Lao Tzu*

Go placidly amid the noise and
haste,
and remember what peace there
may be in silence.
As far as possible without surrender
be on good terms with all persons.
Speak your truth quietly and
clearly;
and listen to others,
even the dull and the ignorant;
they too have their story.

—*Max Ehrmann*

❖

I know what I want, I have
a goal, an opinion, I have a
religion and love. Let me be
myself and then I am satisfied.
I know that I'm a woman, a
woman with inward strength and
plenty of courage.

—*Anne Frank*

❧

Have courage for the great sorrows of life and patience for the small ones; and when you have laboriously accomplished your daily task, go to sleep in peace. God is awake.

—*Victor Hugo*

Notes

_____

_____

_____

_____

_____

_____

_____

_____

_____

_____

_____

_____

_____

❧

❧

.Ruskin Bond.

_____

_____

_____

_____

_____

_____

_____

_____

_____

_____ *.89.*

_____

_____

_____

_____

_____

_____

_____

✤

.90.

❧

.Ruskin Bond.

All glory comes from daring to begin.

Toiling, rejoicing, sorrowing,
Onward through life he goes;
Each morning sees some task
begun,
Each evening sees it close
Something attempted,
something done,
Has earned a night's repose…

Thus at the flaming forge of life
Our fortunes must be wrought;
Thus on its sounding anvil shaped
Each burning deed and thought.

—*H.W. Longfellow*

All art requires infinite patience, skill and dedication. And the greatest reward comes from the very act of taking pains in the pursuit of perfection.

❧

And, on some days, to sit at one's desk is itself an act of bravery. As a pained scribe once remarked: 'Writing is very easy. All you need to do is sit in front of the typewriter until little drops of blood appear on your forehead.'

❧

It is not because things are difficult that we do not dare. It is because we do not dare that they are difficult.

—Seneca

❧

If we want more roses, we must plant more trees!

—George Eliot

❧

.94.

It's setting your eye on the hero
inside,
knowing you're fair to the game.
Knowing you've got what it takes
to be tough
no matter how rough life may be.
I'm a hero, I know it! When my
actions show it
it's because I'm a hero to me. .95.
—*Adeline Foster*

Let me not pray to be sheltered
from dangers,
But to be fearless in facing them.
Let me not beg for the stilling of
my pain,
But for the heart to conquer it…

Grant me that I may not be a
coward,
feeling your mercy in my success
alone,
But let me find the grasp of your
hand in my failure

—*Rabindranath Tagore*

❧

Poorly fed, homesick and struggling in London in the early 1950s, one motto kept me going, 'Never despair. But if you do, work on in despair.' Perhaps it will be a talisman to you, too.

The things I do best are those things which I do on my own, alone, of my own accord, without the advice or approval of others. It is only when I strike out on my own that I succeed best. It has not been easy, but I believe he who has never been afraid has never been brave.

. Ruskin Bond .

Notes

_____

_____

_____

_____

_____

_____

_____

_____

_____

_____

_____

_____

_____

_____

.Ruskin Bond.

_____

_____

_____

_____

_____

_____

_____

_____

_____

_____   *.101.*

_____

_____

_____

_____

_____

_____

_____

_____

❧

.A Little Book of Courage.

.Ruskin Bond.

What a new face courage
puts on everything!

—Ralph Waldo Emerson

Courage was never designed for
show;
It isn't a thing that can come and
go;
It's written in victory and defeat
And every trial a man may meet.
It's part of his hours, his days
and his years,

Back of his smiles and behind his
tears.
Courage is more than a daring
deed:
It's the breath of life and a strong
man's creed.

—Edgar A. Guest

❧

Build castles in the air
But first, give them foundations.
Hold fast to all your dreams,
Make perfect your creations.
All glory comes to those who dare.

Tomorrow's fate, though thou be
wise,
Thou canst not tell yet surmise;
Pass, therefore, not today in vain,
For it will never come again.

—Omar Khayyam

Sweet are the uses of adversity,
Which, like the toad, ugly and
venomous,
Wears yet a precious jewel in his
head.

—*William Shakespeare*

To have courage for whatever
comes in life—everything lies in
that.

—*Mother Teresa*

A man that flies from his fear
may find that he has only taken a
short cut to meet it.

—*J.R.R Tolkien*

Courage is what it takes to stand
up and speak; courage is also
what it takes to sit down and
listen.

—*Winston Churchill*

When you get into a tight place and everything goes against you, till it seems as though you could not hold on a minute longer, never give up then, for that is just the place and time that the tide will turn.

—*Harriet Beecher Stowe*

❦

Don't be afraid of the dark, little
one
Be friends with the Night, there
is nothing to fear.

Says the great Mark Twain, 'To
believe yourself brave is to be
brave; it is the one only essential
thing.'

.Ruskin Bond.

Notes

_____
_____
_____
_____
_____
_____
_____
_____
_____
_____
_____
_____
_____

.111.

❧

.A Little Book of Courage.

❧

.Ruskin Bond.

❧

.A Little Book of Courage.

.Ruskin Bond.

Never look back
    unless you are planning
to go that way.

—Thoreau

The early 1950s; I came back to India from London, and I had no intention of going elsewhere, and as the land was full of all kinds of people of diverse origins, I decided I'd just be myself, all-Indian, even if it meant being a minority of one.

This land is mine
Although I do not own it,
This land is mine
Because I grew upon it.
This dust, this grass,
This tender leaf
And weathered bark
All in my heart are finely blended
Until my time on earth is ended. *.117.*

I prefer to be true to myself, even
at the hazard of incurring the
ridicule of others, rather than to
be false, and to incur my own
abhorrence.

—*Frederick Douglass*

Take for yourself what you can,
and don't be ruled by others; to
belong to oneself—the whole
savour of life lies in that.

—*Ivan Turgenev*

Do one thing at a time, and
do that one thing as if your life
depended upon it.

—*Eugene Grace*

All life is an experiment. The more experiments you make the better. What if they are a little coarse, and you may get your coat soiled or torn? What if you do fail, and get fairly rolled in the dirt once or twice. Up again, you shall never be so afraid of a tumble.

—*Ralph Waldo Emerson*

Life isn't a bed of roses, not for any of us, and I have never had the comforts or luxuries that wealth can provide. But I have done my own thing, in my own time, and my own way. What more can I ask of life?

Each morning when I open my eyes I say to myself: I, not events, have the power to make me happy or unhappy today. I can choose which it shall be. Yesterday is dead, tomorrow hasn't arrived yet. I have just one day, today, and I'm going to be happy.

—*Anonymous*

Notes

_____

_____

_____

_____

_____

_____

_____

_____

_____

_____

_____

_____

❧

❧

.Ruskin Bond.

.A Little Book of Courage.

.Ruskin Bond.

Try again.
Fail again.
Fail better.

—Samuel Beckett

Nothing really worth having comes quickly and easily. If it did, I doubt that we would ever grow.

—*Eknath Easwaran*

Now is no time to think of what
you do not have. Think of what
you can do with what there is.

——*Ernest Hemingway*

If we wait for the moment when
everything, absolutely everything
is ready, we shall never begin.

.129.

——*Ivan Turgenev*

Obstacles are those frightful things you see when you take your eyes off your goal.

—Henry Ford

I never think of the future. It comes soon enough.

—Albert Einstein

I long to accomplish great and noble tasks, but it is my chief duty to accomplish humble tasks as though they were great and noble. The world is moved along, not only by the mighty shoves of its heroes, but also by the aggregate of the tiny pushes of each honest worker. *.131.*

—*Helen Keller*

Great souls have wills; feeble ones have only wishes.

—*A Chinese Proverb*

Not to feel exasperated or defeated or despondent because your days aren't packed with wise and moral actions. But to get back up when you fail, to celebrate behaving like a human—however imperfectly— and fully embrace the pursuit you've embarked on.

—*Marcus Aurelius*

For yesterday is but a dream
And tomorrow is only a vision,
But today well lived makes every
yesterday a dream of happiness
And every tomorrow a vision of
hope.
Look well, therefore, to this day!
Such is the salutation to the dawn.

    —Kalidasa

Out of eternity this new day is
born,
Into eternity at night will return,

Behold it aforetime no eye ever
did;
So soon it forever from all eyes is
hid.

.134. Here hath been dawning another
blue day;
Think, wilt thou let it slip useless
away?

    —Thomas Carlyle

     ❧

Notes

✿

.Ruskin Bond.

.A Little Book of Courage.

_____

_____

_____

_____

_____

_____

_____

_____

_____

_____

_____

_____

_____

.Ruskin Bond.

Keep your face always toward the sunshine—
and shadows will fall behind you.

—Walt Whitman

I like a good sausage, I do;
It's a dish for the chosen and the few.
Oh, for sausage and mash,
And of mustard a dash
And an egg nicely fried—maybe two?

There is something to be said for a good meal to put heart into the most dispiriting of days.

.Ruskin Bond.

Life brings sorrows and joys alike.
It is what a man does with them—
not what they do to him—that is
the true test of his mettle.

—*Theodore Roosevelt*

Adventure—and real courage—
is when a child crawls across the
floor, grabs the leg of a chair, and
stands up for the first time.

.Ruskin Bond.

I would see the old lama, my neighbour, walking past my window and, five minutes later, I would start out on the same road, sure of overtaking him halfway. But, invariably, I would find him standing at the post office when I got there.

The speed of the hare can never match the steady perseverance of the tortoise which never gives up.

❧

If you can't be a pine on the top
of the hill,
Be a scrub in the valley—but be
The best little scrub by the side
of the hill;
Be a bush, if you can't be a tree…

If you can't be a highway, then
just be a trail,
If you can't be the sun, be a star;
It isn't by size that you win or
you fail—
Be the best of whatever you are.

—*Douglas Malloch*

❧

Once we believe in ourselves,
we can risk curiosity, wonder,
spontaneous delight, or any
experience that reveals the
human spirit.

—E.E. Cummings

❧

'Life shrinks or expands in
proportion to one's courage,' says
the writer Anais Nin. Anyone
who has ever been bullied, on
the playground or anywhere else,
would do well to pay heed to her
wise words.

❧

Live! Live the wonderful life that
is in you! Let nothing be lost
upon you. Be always searching
for new sensations. Be afraid of
nothing.

—Oscar Wilde

Notes

_____

_____

_____

_____

_____

.147.

_____

_____

_____

_____

_____

_____

_____

_____

❧

.148.

❧

.Ruskin Bond.

_.149._

.150.

🌿

.Ruskin Bond.

I grant you, sir,
the preacher is an angel
To be a man,
now—that's more difficult

—Ghalib (Trans. Ralph Russell)

It took me a lifetime to come to terms with the loss of my father. You never really get over the loss of a beloved. You learn to live despite it. An acceptance of that which cannot be changed is the true mark of a calm human being.

It is not the mountain we conquer, but ourselves.

—*Sir Edmund Hillary*

It is my joy in life to find
At every turning of the road
The strong arm of a comrade kind
To help me onward with my load.

And since I have no gold to give,
And love alone must make amends,
My only prayer is, while I live—
God make me worthy of my
friends.

—*Frank D. Sherman*

Reflect upon your present blessings—of which every man has many—not on your past misfortunes, of which all men have some.

—*Charles Dickens*

Turn back from the outer, set
your eyes within.

Don't be satisfied with stories,
how things have gone with others.
Unfold your own myth.

—*Rumi*

If I can stop one heart from
breaking,
I shall not live in vain;
If I can ease one life the aching,
Or cool one pain,
Or help one fainting robin
Unto his nest again,
I shall not live in vain.

—*Emily Dickinson*

Give me heart touch with all that
live,
And strength to speak my word;
But if that is denied me, give
The strength to live unheard.

—Edwin Markham

'You yourself, as much as anyone in the entire universe, deserve your love and affection,' says Buddha. Be brave and look within, dear reader, and accept yourself—with all your perfections and imperfections. You will find that the journey of life will go much easier.

And finally, dear reader, a mantra
which has always stood by me.
May it be yours, too:

'This above all, to thine own self
be true,
And it must follow as the night
of the day,
Thou can'st not then be false to
any man.'